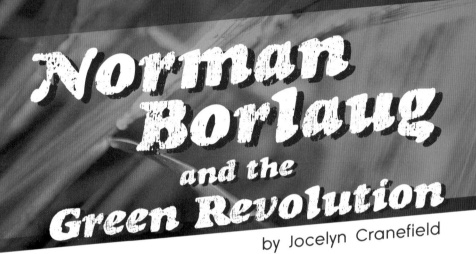

Norman Borlaug and the Green Revolution

by Jocelyn Cranefield

Chapter 1

An Iowa Boy

Norman Borlaug and his friends were on their way to school when they were suddenly caught in a blizzard. Norman became exhausted from walking in the wind and cold. He decided to lie down in the deep, soft snow, telling the others he couldn't go on.

His cousin Sina grabbed him, shouting that he had to keep moving. Her actions made him get back up. By not letting him stop and sleep in the blizzard, she had saved his life. Years later, Norman said that Sina's refusal to let him give up continued to inspire him as an adult.

Norman Borlaug had to walk to school in all kinds of weather.

Norman was born in Saude, Iowa, in 1914. He was the eldest of four children. People in this farming community relied on the land to survive, and from a young age, Norman had work to do. He helped raise cattle, pigs, and chickens, and to grow oats and corn.

At the one-room school, the children began each day by singing "The Iowa Corn Song." In the winter, there were 16 students, but in the summer, there were only 10 or 12. The students were needed to help harvest the crops.

GIVING 105%

During high school, Norman took up baseball and wrestling. His wrestling coach always encouraged him to "give 105%." This helped him develop a toughness and strength that he would call on later in life.

Norman Borlaug was made a member of the National Wrestling Hall of Fame in 1992.

When Norman finished high school, his grandfather encouraged him to keep studying. Borlaug enrolled at the University of Minnesota, taking odd jobs to help pay his way. This was during the **Great Depression**. Borlaug was shocked to meet many desperate, hungry people who had lost their jobs, savings, and property.

One day in college, he heard a scientist talk about microscopic **fungus** spores called rust, which feed on crops and destroy them. The scientist, Dr. Elvin Stakman, argued that if science could find a way to help plants resist rust, world hunger would be reduced. Borlaug was instantly hooked on the idea. He went on to study with Dr. Stakman.

This wheat stem has rust. Microscopic rust spores are picked up by the wind and carried from plant to plant.

Chapter 2

Borlaug Goes to Mexico

When he finished college, Borlaug got a job with the DuPont chemical company. Two years later, his former teacher, Dr. Stakman, encouraged him to join a project working on solving Mexico's food shortage problem.

Mexico needed more food to feed its **population**. Borlaug's job was to lead a team of scientists and farmers. They needed to figure out how to grow more wheat on each acre of farmland, increasing the land's **yield**.

YIELD

The only part of wheat used for food is the seed, or grain. Yield is the amount of grain that comes from an area planted with wheat. The yield depends on how many heads of wheat there are, the number of seeds, and the size of the seeds. The better the yield, the more people can be fed.

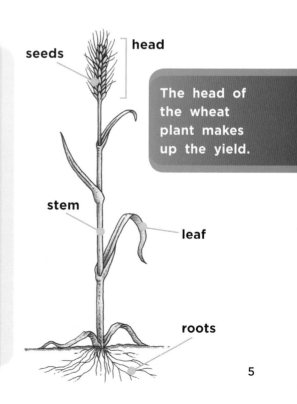

seeds

head

The head of the wheat plant makes up the yield.

stem

leaf

roots

There was another problem: much of Mexico's wheat crop was being ruined by rust fungus. Borlaug needed to breed wheat that resisted rust. This could take 10 to 12 years using normal methods.

Borlaug started his work at the Yaqui *(YAH-kee)* Valley farm **research** station in Sonora, Mexico. The conditions there were perfect for growing wheat. It was warm and sunny, the soil was fertile, and the land was irrigated.

Borlaug had a theory about how to double the rate of breeding wheat, but it meant breaking with tradition. At that time, scientists normally bred plants in a single location. This made it easy to control the growing conditions and compare the results of experiments. Scientists also thought that newly harvested seeds needed a rest, to store energy, before being planted.

The Yaqui Valley was a good place to grow wheat in the winter, but in the summer it was too hot. If Borlaug could find somewhere else to grow wheat in the summer, he could run his experiments all year long.

The Yaqui Valley is sometimes called the home of the "green revolution" because of Norman Borlaug's work there.

Chapter 3
A Breakthrough

Borlaug was energetic and traveled all around Mexico. He was looking for places where wheat would grow in the summer. In the cold, mountain climate of the south, he found two sites near each other that seemed perfect: Toluca *(toh-LEW-kah)* Valley and Chapingo *(chah-PEEN-goh)*.

WHEAT-BREEDING SITES IN MEXICO

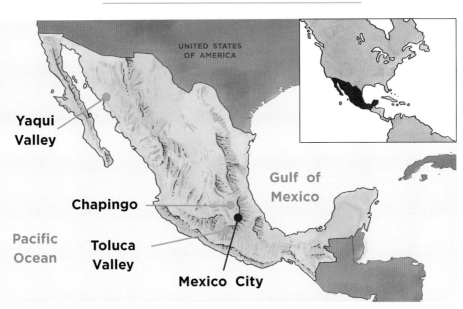

Now Borlaug had two different growing seasons to work with. He could grow wheat in the Yaqui Valley in the winter, and the Toluca Valley and Chapingo in the summer.

With the help of local farmers, Borlaug set about **crossbreeding** different kinds of wheat. Each time a new **generation** of plants grew in the Yaqui Valley, he spent hours continuing his observation.

He took notes on the plants' size, how fast they grew, and their resistance to disease. He picked the best plants and crossed them with other successful plants, creating a new generation to grow at the southern sites.

Borlaug's theory had proved correct. By moving plants between sites with different growing seasons, he could do twice as many breeding experiments. He had doubled the breeding rate of the wheat in his program.

Norman Borlaug (third from left) with a group of Mexican farmers in a wheat field.

All this testing helped Borlaug and his team develop a **strain** of wheat that resisted disease. They were excited about the disappearance of the rust, but they found a new problem. The plants bent over from the weight of their own grain.

They started using shorter plants, called dwarfs, in the breeding program. The strong, thick stems of these wheat plants helped them to stay upright, and they produced more grain. By crossing the dwarf plants with the taller wheat, Borlaug's team developed a new variety of wheat that resisted disease and had short, strong stems.

Norman Borlaug shows two varieties of wheat.

Norman Borlaug's work in Mexico took more than fifteen years, but it was a huge success. In the end, he bred more than 40 short, rust-resistant strains of high-yield wheat. When the new strains were grown with fertilizer, they produced two to three times more grain than normal wheat.

His system of breeding had another benefit, too. The new wheat had been grown in different climates, with different numbers of daylight hours, making it tough and adaptable. This was good news for the rest of the world.

MEXICO'S WHEAT YIELDS BEFORE AND AFTER
THE HIGH-YIELD SEMI-DWARF VARIETY

Wheat yield in 1945:
about 250,000 tons

Wheat yield in 1965:
about 2,500,000 tons

After the new wheat strains were planted throughout Mexico, the wheat yield increased by four times between 1945 and 1956. Between 1945 and 1965, there was an increase of ten times in 20 years!

Chapter 4
More Wheat for the World

In the 1960s, Norman Borlaug turned his attention to an even bigger problem. India and Pakistan were struggling to produce enough food for their growing populations. Many scientists believed that millions of people could starve.

Borlaug shipped hundreds of tons of the new wheat seeds to India and Pakistan and explained to government officials how to grow them.

MEXICO, INDIA, AND PAKISTAN

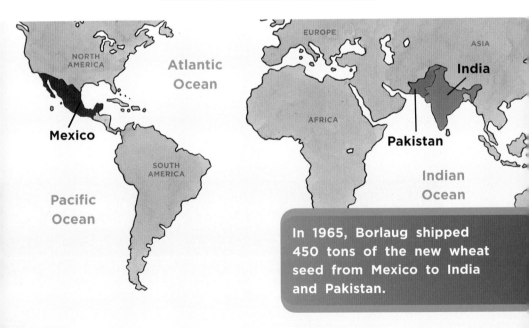

In 1965, Borlaug shipped 450 tons of the new wheat seed from Mexico to India and Pakistan.

Within a few years, the new types of wheat were growing across many parts of India and Pakistan. Yields increased remarkably. Between 1964 and 2001, Pakistan's wheat production increased from 4.5 to 22 million tons. India's increased from 12 to 75 million tons!

It wasn't just Borlaug's seeds that spread. His ideas started to migrate, too. In a flurry of growth, plant-breeding stations were set up in India, Pakistan, Canada, the United States, and South America by the late 1960s.

Scientists in these places began working together as a community. They shared test results and sent each other seeds. They changed their behaviors: it was a whole new way of working.

The high-yield wheat grew quickly, but it needed a lot of water and nutrients. Borlaug encouraged farmers to change their traditional practices and start using **irrigation** and fertilizer. Together, the new plants and these new farming methods were called the "green revolution."

Borlaug taught Indian scientists and farmers about the new wheat.

Early one morning in 1970, the phone rang. Borlaug had already left for work, so his wife drove after him to share the news. He was in a wheat field when he learned that he had won the Nobel Peace Prize. Nobody had ever won it for growing plants before!

THE BLUE REVOLUTION

Before he died, at age 95, Norman Borlaug also became concerned about a future world shortage of water. He called for a "blue revolution" to conserve water.

Norman Borlaug is credited with saving a billion lives. His innovations transformed farming and helped people see that science and technology could lead to improvements in farming. He also helped to build a global community of scientists who could work together on solving problems.

Borlaug's new ideas helped people all over the world.

14

Respond to Reading

Summarize

Use important details from *Norman Borlaug and the Green Revolution* to summarize how Norman Borlaug investigated his questions about nature. Your graphic organizer may help you.

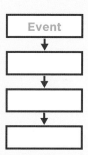

Text Evidence

1. How do you know that *Norman Borlaug and the Green Revolution* is a biography? Give examples from the text. GENRE

2. In Chapter 1, what was the sequence of events that led Borlaug to work as a plant scientist? SEQUENCE

3. The suffix *-ic* means "of or like something." For example, adding *-ic* to the noun *metal* forms the adjective *metallic*, meaning "made of or looking like metal." What does *microscopic* on page 4 mean? GREEK AND LATIN SUFFIXES

4. Reread Chapter 4. Write about the sequence of events that increased wheat production in India and Pakistan. WRITE ABOUT READING

Compare Texts

Read a traditional story that shows the importance of observing nature.

Golden Apples

Each year, Lady Setenaya noticed a special apple growing at the top of her golden apple tree. This apple was very different from the other apples. It took longer to grow than the rest. It was also larger, rounder, and firmer when it ripened. But when fall came, the special apple slowly shrank again.

Patiently, Lady Setenaya watched and waited. When the first frost came, she picked the apple while it was still ripe and juicy.

Over several years, Lady Setenaya tested different uses for the apple and carefully observed the results.

She found that if people bit into its flesh, they became kinder, younger, and more energetic. If she mashed its core into a cream, it made people's skin soft and radiant. And when she boiled the skin, those who drank the broth became joyful.

News of the special apple spread. One day, a disease called Cholera disguised itself as an old man and came to her, begging for a taste. Lady Setenaya's powers of observation had grown sharp, and she saw through his trickery.

She knew that Cholera would kill more people if he became younger, and so she turned him away. Very angry, he crept back at night and cut down the tree.

Lady Setenaya was very upset. However, she found that she no longer needed the golden apple. Her years of studying nature and observing people had made her a talented natural physician. Very soon she discovered new ways to keep her people healthy and happy.

 ## Make Connections

How did Lady Setenaya use observation to investigate questions about nature?
ESSENTIAL QUESTION

What role do time and the seasons play when investigating questions about nature? Use examples from *Norman Borlaug and the Green Revolution* and *Golden Apples* to support your answer.
TEXT TO TEXT

Glossary

crossbreeding *(KRAWS-breed-ing)* combining elements of two or more plants or animals to make something new *(page 9)*

fungus *(FUN-guhs)* a plant-like organism that survives by breaking down other plants and animals *(page 4)*

generation *(jen-uh-RAY-shuhn)* a single step in the ancestry of people, plants, or animals *(page 9)*

Great Depression *(GRAYT di-PRESH-uhn)* a worldwide economic downturn from 1929 to 1939 *(page 4)*

irrigation *(ir-uh-GAY-shuhn)* a system of supplying water to crops *(page 13)*

population *(pop-yuh-LAY-shuhn)* the number of people who live in a country, city, or region *(page 5)*

research *(ri-SURCH)* studying to better understand something *(page 6)*

strain *(strayn)* a variety with ancestors in common *(page 10)*

yield *(yeeld)* the amount produced *(page 5)*

Index

Focus on Science

Purpose To find out what happens when plants are crossbred

Procedure

Step 1 ▶ Research real hybrid plants that have been crossbred for specific traits.

Step 2 ▶ Pick two of the plants that you want to know more about. Make sure you identify the traits for which they were bred and why.

Step 3 ▶ For each plant, make a family tree that shows the ancestors and the resulting hybrid. Label each of the ancestors and include their attributes. Make sure you also include the hybrid's attributes.

Step 4 ▶ Share your plant family trees with the class. Explain why you chose your plants and why your hybrid is important.

Conclusion What have you learned about crossbreeding plants? Is crossbreeding always successful? Why or why not? How does crossbreeding help us? If you were going to crossbreed plants, what would you crossbreed? Why? Explain your choices.